Guinea Pig

A Fun and Educational Book for Kids with Amazing Facts and Pictures

Table of Contents

Introduction

Cavy, or guinea pigs, are domesticated rodents that are sometimes kept as pets. They were initially tamed by the Inca people and are indigenous to the Andes Mountains in South America. The body of a guinea pig is small, spherical, and has short legs but no tail. Since they are gregarious creatures, they frequently coexist in packs in the wild.

Guinea pigs are well-known for being calm and kind as pets, and they can be wonderful friends for both kids and adults. They require a balanced diet of hay, green vegetables, and pellets and are simple to care for. Also, guinea pigs require a tidy home space with lots of room for running about and playing.

Guinea pigs come in a variety of breeds, such as the American, Abyssinian, Peruvian, and Teddy varieties, each having a distinctive coat and set of traits. For those who are prepared to give them the right care and attention, guinea pigs may make delightful, low-maintenance pets with a lifetime of about 5-7 years.

Scientific Name

Cavia porcellus is the guinea pig's scientific name.

Appearance

The body of a guinea pig is small, spherical, and has short legs but no tail. They normally range in size from 8 to 10 inches (20 to 25 cm) long and weigh between 450 and 3 pounds (450–1360 grams).

Both solid hues like white, black, brown, and cream as well as multicolored patterns like tortoiseshell, brindle, and calico are among the possible hues and patterns for their fur. The Abyssinian has short, coarse hair that grows in rosettes or swirls, while other guinea pig breeds, including the Peruvian and Silkie, have long, flowing fur.

Large, round eyes and small, usually covered-by-fur ears are features of guinea pigs. They must nibble on hay or other items to prevent their front teeth from getting too long because they are constantly growing.

Geography

Guinea pigs are indigenous to South America's Andes Mountains, more especially Peru, Ecuador, and Colombia. Around 5,000 years ago, the Incas tamed them and used them for food and ceremonial purposes.

Guinea pigs can now be found in the wild and as domestic pets all over the world. They are frequently bred for display or as companion animals and are well-liked pets in many nations, including the United States, the United Kingdom, and Australia. Guinea pigs often live in groups in burrows or nests and can be found in grasslands, woodlands, and rocky places in the wild.

Behavior

Although guinea pigs are gregarious creatures that do best in groups, they can also be kept as solitary pets if they receive a lot of human contact and attention. They are awake during the day and only sleep for little durations at night.

Guinea pigs are often calm, amiable, and they want to be around people. When touched or held, they frequently squeak or purr. They may even learn to know their owner's voice and respond when called. Nonetheless, it's crucial to handle them softly and quietly because they might be easily startled by rapid movements or loud noises.

The vocalizations of guinea pigs, which include a variety of squeaks, chirps, and purrs, are also well recognized. They may use various noises to express their feelings or to signal hunger, thirst, or pain.

Guinea pigs enjoy playing with toys including chew toys, balls, and tunnels as well as exploring their surroundings. They also enjoy eating and will graze on hay, fresh produce, and pellets for a large portion of the day.

In general, guinea pigs are wonderful pets if their owners are prepared to provide them the necessary love, care, and socialization.

Reproduction

Although it's advised to wait at least three months before mating, guinea pigs attain sexual maturity at roughly three to five weeks of age. The gestation period for female guinea pigs (sows) ranges from 63 to 70 days, and they can get pregnant at any moment.

Boars will frequently conduct a "rumble strut" and a sequence of vocalizations to attract females during courtship. When a female is ready to mate, it happens swiftly and can be rather raucous.

During a few weeks, a sow will start to exhibit signs of pregnancy, like as weight gain, a bigger tummy, and decreased activity. At this period, it's crucial to give the sow a lot of food, water, and a nice place to live.

Although larger litters are conceivable, guinea pigs normally have litters of 1-6 puppies. The puppies can start eating solid food in a few of days after they are born completely furred, with open eyes. Before the puppies are weaned, the mother will nurse them for about three to four weeks.

Guinea pigs may breed rapidly and easily, therefore it's advised to keep males and females apart unless you plan to actively breed them. Health problems and overcrowding in their living space might result from overpopulation.

Social Life

Since they prefer to be in groups, guinea pigs are social animals. They frequently live in herds or groups of up to 10 people in the wild, and they interact with one another by using a range of vocalizations and body language.

To avoid fighting and promote socializing, guinea pigs should ideally be kept as pets in pairs or small groups of the same sex. To avoid violent behavior, it's crucial to introduce new guinea pigs to an established group gradually and under strict supervision.

The frequent grooming of guinea pigs is a sign of affection and social bonding. Also, they might share a bedtime kiss and interact with toys or other objects.

It's crucial to provide guinea pigs regular human contact and attention in addition to allowing them to engage with other animals. To make them feel safe and content, this can involve handling, petting, and playing with them on a daily basis.

Guinea pigs are, in general, social creatures who require a lot of socialization and engagement to survive. They can make excellent and satisfying pets if you give them a suitable living space, the right care, and attention.

Habitat

Although they can be maintained as pets both indoors and outside, guinea pigs need a secure and cozy home with lots of room to roam and explore.

Habitats for guinea pigs indoors often consist of a cage or enclosure with a stable floor, sufficient ventilation, and enough room for them to move around without restriction. The cage you select for your guinea pigs should be big enough for their size and the quantity you intend to keep, and you should give them lots of bedding, toys, and hiding places.

In addition to offering the guinea pigs lots of room to roam and play, outdoor habitats like hutches or runs should also shield them from predators, harsh weather, and direct sunlight. It's crucial to give children a safe environment devoid of potential threats including toxic plants, sharp objects, and other risks.

In order to stay healthy and happy, guinea pigs need access to fresh water, hay, and a balanced diet of pellets and fresh produce, whether they are kept indoors or outside. In order to avoid the accumulation of waste and bacteria, they also need their living space cleaned on a regular basis.

Ultimately, guinea pigs' physical and social needs must be met in a safe, comfortable living space if they are to be healthy and happy.

Senses

A variety of senses that guinea pigs possess enable them to interact with one another and navigate their surroundings.

Sight: Guinea pigs can see in color and recognize motion, and they have generally healthy eyes. They can see about 340 degrees around their body and have a broad field of vision.

Hearing: Guinea pigs have great hearing and are able to distinguish high-pitched noises that are inaudible to humans. They can hear and maybe respond to the ultrasonic noises made by other animals and employ a range of vocalizations to communicate with one another.

Smell: Guinea pigs can communicate with one another and traverse their surroundings because to their highly developed sense of smell. They have an acute sense of smell that aids in finding food and identifying potential threats.

Touch: Guinea pigs use their highly developed sense of touch and sensitive whiskers to explore their surroundings and communicate with one another. They might also groom or cuddle you as a way to express their affection through touch.

Taste: Guinea pigs are capable of detecting bitter, sour, and sweet flavors. They are herbivores and mainly rely on taste to find and recognize food.

Overall, guinea pigs have a variety of senses that enable them to communicate with one another and traverse their environment, which makes them well-adapted to both life as pets and their natural habitat.

Feeding

Since they are herbivores, guinea pigs need a diet rich in fiber and vitamin C. The following food items should be included in a guinea pig's diet:

Hay: Hay should comprise the majority of a guinea pig's diet because it is a crucial component of their nutrition. The best choices are timothy hay, orchard grass hay, and meadow hay.

Pellets: Pellets should be used sparingly and be created especially for guinea pigs. Pellets offer extra vitamins and nutrients that may not be present in hay alone.

Vegetables: Guinea pigs should be provided with a daily diet that includes a range of fresh vegetables, such as bell peppers, carrots, cucumbers, and leafy greens like kale, spinach, and lettuce. Vegetables should be introduced gradually to prevent causing upset stomachs.

Fruits: Although they contain a lot of sugar and should only be consumed occasionally, fruits can offer variety and health to a guinea pig's diet. Strawberries, pears, and apples are all healthy fruit options.

Water: Guinea pigs should always have access to fresh, clean water. Water should be changed everyday to stop the growth of bacteria.

Avoid giving guinea pigs items that are harmful to them, such chocolate, coffee, and avocado, as well as foods that are heavy in sugar, fat, or salt. It's crucial to keep an eye on their food intake and give them lots of exercise and opportunities to move around because overfeeding can also result in health issues.

Diet

A guinea pig's general health and wellbeing depend on having a balanced diet. Since they are herbivores, guinea pigs need a diet rich in fiber, vitamin C, and food that is low in fat and sugar. These are some recommendations for a wholesome diet for guinea pigs:

Hay: Hay should comprise the majority of a guinea pig's diet because it is a crucial component of their nutrition. It gives them the fiber they require to maintain a healthy digestive tract and aids in removing the enamel from their constantly erupting teeth. Good choices include timothy hay, orchard grass hay, and meadow hay.

Pellets: Provide pellets in moderation and make sure they are made exclusively for guinea pigs. Pellets offer extra vitamins and nutrients that may not be present in hay alone. Do not feed them pellets made for rabbits or chinchillas, since these may not fulfill the unique dietary requirements of guinea pigs.

Vegetables: Guinea pigs should be provided with a daily diet that includes a range of fresh vegetables, such as bell peppers, carrots, cucumbers, and leafy greens like kale, spinach, and lettuce. Vegetables should be introduced gradually to prevent causing upset stomachs.

Fruits: Due to their high sugar content, fruits should only be consumed in moderation. Strawberries, pears, and apples are all healthy fruit options.

Water: Guinea pigs should always have access to fresh, clean water. Water should be changed every day to stop the growth of bacteria.

Avoid giving guinea pigs items that are harmful to them, such chocolate, coffee, and avocado, as well as foods that are heavy in sugar, fat, or salt. It's crucial to keep an eye on their food intake and give them lots of exercise and opportunities to move around because overfeeding can also result in health issues.

Babies

Puppies, as guinea pigs are known, are born completely furred and with their eyes open. Guinea pigs can have litters of one to six young, on average two to four, and their gestation period is between 59 to 72 days.

Within a few hours of birth, newborn guinea pigs may move around and suck from their mother and weigh between 70 and 100 grams. Within the first week, they should be introduced to hay and pellets as they will begin to eat solid food.

To avoid unintended breeding, male and female puppies must be separated by three weeks of age. Between three and four weeks of age, puppies should also be weaned from their mothers and given their own cage.

Baby guinea pigs need to be given a warm and cozy habitat, clean water, and food, as well as regular growth and development checks. To help them socialize and feel at ease around people, it's also crucial to handle them gently and regularly.

Predators

Guinea pigs have a wide variety of predators in the wild. Birds of prey like hawks and eagles, wild cats like foxes and bobcats, snakes, and certain larger mammals like dogs and coyotes are a few of the common predators of guinea pigs.

Guinea pigs are frequently kept as pets inside or in secure cages, which lowers their danger of being attacked by predators. They may still be vulnerable to assault by other home pets like cats or dogs, so it's crucial to make sure their surroundings is safe and secure.

It's crucial to give guinea pigs a safe, predator-proof environment while housing them outside, including a roof or covering to stop raptors from swooping down and attacking the animals. In addition, strong materials that can survive attempts by predators to break in should be used to construct outdoor enclosures.

Evolution

The family Caviidae, which comprises various South American-native rodent species, includes guinea pigs. Guinea pigs' origins can be traced to the Andean region of South America, where the local populace domesticated their wild predecessors for use in food and rituals.

The first guinea pigs that were domesticated were probably raised for their flesh and fur as well as for ceremonial purposes. They later spread to other regions of the world, including North America, after becoming well-liked pets in Europe.

The physical evolution of guinea pigs has not changed significantly throughout time. They still resemble little, spherical rodents with short legs and fur. Because their herbivorous diet, which is heavy in fiber and necessitates specialized digestive organs to break down and process, there is evidence to suggest that their digestive systems have evolved over time.

Overall, guinea pigs' intimate interaction with humans, who have selectively bred them for particular uses and introduced them to new locations outside of their original range, has affected their evolution.

Population

It is challenging to estimate the guinea pig population because they are frequently kept as pets and are not frequently counted in wildlife surveys. Guinea pigs are still frequently kept for food and as a source of revenue in their native South America, nonetheless.

In some regions of South America, there are also wild populations of guinea pigs, though it is unknown how many there are there and where they are located. Due to habitat degradation and poaching, several wild guinea pig species, like the wild cavy (Cavia aperea), are regarded as fragile or threatened.

Guinea pigs make popular pets because of their small size, friendliness, and ease of care. They are frequently bred for sale in pet stores and online, where they are frequently kept in couples or small groups. To maintain their health and wellness, it's crucial to make sure that pet guinea pigs are purchased from reliable sources and that their care requirements are satisfied.

Conservation Status

As they are often raised and maintained as pets all over the world, guinea pigs are not regarded as a threatened or endangered species. However, due to habitat degradation, hunting, and competition with introduced species, some wild guinea pig species, including the wild cavy (Cavia aperea), are regarded as vulnerable or threatened.

The primary goals of conservation efforts for wild guinea pigs are to safeguard their natural habitats and stop further ecological degradation. Several groups also try to foster ethical hunting methods and to persuade local communities to value and safeguard wild guinea pig populations.

Guinea pigs are not often included in conservation efforts because they are kept as pets, but it is still crucial for owners to exercise responsible pet ownership, get their animals from trustworthy sources, and provide them with the right care and surroundings. This can lessen the demand for guinea pigs that are caught in the wild and safeguard their natural populations.

Health

Although guinea pigs are typically healthy creatures, they are prone to some health issues like any pets. The following are a few of the most typical health conditions that might afflict guinea pigs:

Dental issues: Because guinea pigs' teeth are constantly growing, they may experience dental issues, such as overgrown teeth, which can hurt and make eating challenging.

Infections of the respiratory system are common in guinea pigs and may be brought on by bacteria or viruses. Sneezing, coughing, wheezing, and drainage from the nose or eyes are signs of a respiratory infection.

Many internal and external parasites, including mites, lice, and worms, can harm guinea pigs.

Constipation, diarrhea, and bloating are among the digestive issues that guinea pigs are susceptible to due to their sensitive digestive systems.

Overfeeding and inactivity can make guinea pigs obese, which raises their risk of developing conditions like arthritis and heart disease.

It's critical to provide your guinea pig a well-balanced food, lots of exercise, and frequent veterinary checkups if you want to keep them healthy. Also, you should keep their living space tidy and give them access to an abundance of hay and fresh water. It's critical to seek medical care straight away if your guinea pig exhibits any symptoms of disease or strange behavior.

Lifespan

Guinea pigs normally live 4-6 years on average, though some can live even longer with the right care. The length of a guinea pig's life can be influenced by a variety of variables, including genetics, nutrition, and environment.

It's crucial to remember that different illnesses and health issues, including tumors, respiratory infections, and dental issues, can affect a guinea pig's longevity. Regular veterinary exams and the right treatment can help guarantee that your guinea pig lives a healthy and happy life.

Conclusion

Popular pets recognized for their charming and amiable personalities are guinea pigs. They are relatively simple to care for and gregarious animals who prefer the company of others of their own kind. Guinea pigs are often maintained as pets all over the world, but they may also be found in the wild in some regions of South America, where they serve as a vital source of food and revenue for the area's residents.

The various morphological and behavioral traits that distinguish guinea pigs from other animals. They are herbivores and need a diet rich in fiber. Moreover, because their teeth are constantly developing, they need to be worn down to prevent dental issues. As social creatures, guinea pigs develop strong ties with both their owners and other guinea pigs.

As with any pet, it's crucial to provide your guinea pig the right attention and care to maintain their wellbeing. This entails giving them a balanced diet, a clean living space, and routine veterinarian exams. Guinea pigs can have long, healthy lives as cherished pets if given the right care.